Fascism in
21st Century
America...
...its causes and effects

By Jim Boeglin

Author's Tranquility Press
MARIETTA, GEORGIA

Jim Boeglin/Author's Tranquility Press
2706 Station Club Drive SW
Marietta, GA 30060
www.authorstranquilitypress.com

Ordering Information:
Quantity sales. Special discounts are available on quantity purchases by corporations, associations, and others. For details, contact the "Special Sales Department" at the address above.

Fascism in 21st Century America/Jim Boeglin
Paperback: 978-1-958554-81-4
eBook: 978-1-958554-82-1

America's 21st Century Dilemma:

Do We Choose Fear-Based Authoritarianism?

Shall we see a fearful world
Where cruel fascism thrives
With swastika flags unfurled
To control our fear-filled lives?
History has seen the scare
Of authoritarian rule
That leaves the people in despair,
With fear its gruesome tool.

Or

Do We Choose Love-Based Freedom?

The Founders of our Nation
Were wise beyond their years,
Knowing each generation
Would be tested by new fears.
Democracy protects the rights
Of people everywhere,
Turning darkness into light,
With freedoms we all share.

Contents

Part Three. Responses to the Threat of Fascism in America

Acknowledgments

The fate of journalists and protestors in Russia during Putin's brutal invasion of Ukraine are a timely reminder of the shadow that fascism casts over freedoms that most Americans still take for granted. Thousands of journalists and demonstrators have been arrested and jailed in Russia for expressing their opposition to this illegal, cruel, and inhumane invasion.

Americans are not somehow immune to government suppression of constitutionally guaranteed freedoms. Freedom of the press, free speech, religious freedom, due process, and the right to peacefully assemble in protest of governmental policies, are not automatic. Like muscles, they need continuous exercise in order to remain strong. In an autocratic atmosphere, democratic rights and freedoms tend to atrophy.

It seems America is currently on the edge, teetering between a future of a free and democratically-elected, representative form of government, or one of authoritarianism. This book gratefully acknowledges all of the journalists and leaders who are actively involved in keeping democracy alive, and holding fascism at bay, in 21st Century America.

Preliminary Thoughts

I do not consider myself a scholar of either history or politics in the traditional sense. I was an economics major who also took American and European history courses during my time at Indiana University in the 1960s. Over the years I have read numerous books on the human, personal tragedies of WWI and WWII. Law School delved into the history of English Common Law, the development of American governmental and judicial systems, State and Federal laws, Rules of Civil and Criminal Procedure, and the United States Constitution and its court challenges.

Aside from this formal education, I was born on February 2, 1943--the date of a major turning point in WWII—and have personally lived roughly four/fifths of a century of history and politics with my eyes at least partially open.

It is with these meager credentials that I write about my understanding of fascism and its threat to the America so many of us know and love. I consider myself to be a volunteer member of the fire brigade, helping to douse the flames of fascism before they burn down democracy in America.

If we are open to learning, I believe that everyone is our teacher and every moment is a teaching moment. Every person alive has a purpose in the grand scheme of things. There is a dark side and a light side to everyone, and we are all struggling to teach and to learn to be better human beings.

Most of us are consistently striving to distance ourselves from the dark side, and move in the direction of our "Better Angels". A few of us seem to be temporarily fixated on the ego and the dark side. In my opinion, that does not make such people evil, but perhaps damaged, misguided, and a danger to the rest of society. They have chosen a difficult, angry, joyless role in the Divine Plan. As with criminal activities, civil society may need protection from their dangerous intentions and cruel behaviors.

Our greatest teachers are often the people we find most difficult, with lessons we might prefer not to have to learn. However, difficult people and challenging situations can also provide our strongest growth opportunities. Lessons often come from unexpected sources.

It is in this spirit that I acknowledge former President Donald J. Trump and his followers. Trumpism is a movement that encompasses elements of authoritarianism, totalitarianism, despotism, fascism, racism, sexism, nativism, xenophobism, anarchism, bourgeoiseism, populism, evangelism, nationalism, terrorism, egoism, narcissism, cynicism, conservatism, capitalism, prevaricationism, and propagandism. It is a smorgasbord of misguided values.

Trumpism has played an important role in exposing, unleashing, nourishing, and misleading the previously underground fascist forces at work in America. These misguided, fearful, and angry racists existed in America long before Donald J. Trump charged onto the political scene, but as president he gave them credibility, permission, and coaxed them out from hiding to become an important part of his active support and voter base. There are lessons to be learned from Trumpism whether the rest of us like it or not.

I believe that former President Trump will go down in history as one of America's greatest teachers. He has already taught many of his devoted followers that:

- It is acceptable—even admirable--to be angry, prejudiced, hateful, disrespectful, cruel, void of empathy, and uncivil within a supposedly civil society. These shocking character traits represent strength and power deserving of emulation;

- Violence and personal attacks are appropriate if/when Trump encourages them;
- America's electoral system is rigged and dishonest—but only if Trump loses;
- A strong, autocratic leader is preferable to a bunch of wishy-washy elected legislators or the "deep state" for governing a nation;
- Wealth is a great measure of intelligence;
- Trump has both wealth and a genius IQ, which entitles him to unlimited power;
- As President he was/is above the law;
- Government officials, the military, Trump's advisors, his base, and members of his political party have an undivided duty of loyalty to Trump personally, rather than to America, the rule of law, or the Constitution;
- America would be great again if only we could go back to the good old days--of segregation, Jim Crow voting practices, when women belonged in the home, white men were in charge, strong-arm tactics from police were expected and admired, vigilante justice prevailed with impunity, a strong military dictated foreign policy, and businesses operated free of governmental regulations;
- America should go it alone in the world without the interference or participation of our traditional allies;

- NATO is an unneeded and irrelevant "rip-off" of America's taxpayers;
- A kick-ass military is all we need to be the dominant power in the world;
- Despite being a draft-dodger, Trump knows more about the military than the generals and admirals;
- He knows more about COVID-19 than the scientists and medical community;
- There is a "deep state" within the Federal government that is out to steal our souls;
- The free press is the enemy of the people;
- Climate change and COVID are liberal hoaxes;
- Russia's dictator is a better source of intelligence than the entire U.S. Intelligence Community; and
- He alone can fix every problem facing America in the 21st-Century.

The less than devoted followers of Donald Trump, and the "Never Trumpers", have learned important lessons as well:

- Fear, anger, ignorance, and hatred are powerful and destructive energies;
- A leader with a narcissistic personality disorder can create chaotic and dangerous conditions for the nation and the world;

- Lies, deceptions, and unfounded conspiracy theories become the new reality if repeated often enough, loud enough, and long enough;
- For some, truth is an irrelevant inconvenience;
- Blatant hypocrisy has become an acceptable form of political leadership;
- Treasured institutions such as The Justice Department (including the FBI), U.S. Military, Federal Reserve, Treasury, Homeland Security, Environmental Protection, the Intelligence Community, Congress, and the Federal Judiciary can be weaponized to support an autocratic leader's personal agenda;
- Trump prefers the company of authoritarian dictators to duly elected democratic leaders, and admires their aggressive and illegal actions such as Putin's "ingenious" invasion and brutal destruction of neighboring Ukraine;
- He has the charismatic ability to lead a common cult of such diverse groups as Evangelical Christians, radical white supremacists, QAnon conspirators, America Firsters, anti-maskers, anti-vaxxers, Holocaust deniers, opponents of critical race theory, vigilante law and order proponents, book banners, gun rights activists, fascists, and vote suppressors—all with an angry, fear-based message;

- Private/religious schools are a preferable alternative to the "liberal-controlled" public school system and should be supported by American taxpayers at the expense of the public schools;
- Critical thinking has no place in the school curriculum or any other educational setting;
- Critical Race Theory is a threat to the well-documented white history of America;
- The Constitutional concept of separation of church and state is obsolete;
- Churches can be used to impose their version of morality on the American people, even if church dogma discriminates against many people;
- Elections can be manipulated to get the desired results; and
- Our more than two-century-old democratic system of government is a lot more fragile than we previously thought.

An autocratic president who considers himself above the rule of law is demonstrating classic fascist tendencies. Trump's bullying, fear tactics, attacks on the press and anyone who disagrees with him, and apparent inability to recognize or acknowledge the truth, are a reminder of McCarthyism of the 1950s. As with Senator Joseph McCarthy, Trump has enlisted the support of weak and opportunistic party leaders to spread his gospel of hate and suppress the vulnerable opposition. McCarthyism and Trumpism are cut from the same cloth and pose fascist threats to our democracy.

This book is dedicated to my fellow travelers who consistently choose light over darkness; love over fear; kindness over mean-spiritedness; sharing over greed; humility over arrogance; integrity over deception; respect over rudeness; unity over divisiveness; peace over violence; and forgiveness over hatred. Collectively, we are America's best hope for the future of our democracy.

Introduction

"The secret of freedom lies in educating people, whereas the secret of tyranny is in keeping them ignorant." Maximilien Robespierre

Democracy is a participatory form of government. It requires strong, independent-minded, well-intentioned and informed citizens who are able to reason, critically think, and act in an enlightened way. In comparison, autocracies flourish with citizens who willingly obey orders about what to think and what to do, turning a blind eye to any cruelty or injustice engendered by the anger, fear, or hatred behind those orders.

Throughout the long history of this experiment in American Democracy, I suspect a significant minority of Americans have secretly held a favorable view of authoritarianism. It seems that some Americans would actually prefer a benevolent, autocratic dictator to the "messy" representative form of government created by our Founders.

Dictatorships cut short the decision-making process. Putin's decision to invade Ukraine is a perfect example of authoritarian action. A dictator does not have to consider diverse points of view or compromise in order to persuade a majority to accept the plan, thereby making decisions simpler, easier, more decisive, and more efficient. There is no consensus building; no checks and balances in an authoritarian regime.

Growing up Catholic, I can relate to this autocratic perspective. I was indoctrinated to feel guilty for questioning the teachings of the Church--such as being tainted with Original Sin, being an unworthy sinner, males-only in charge, and the infallibility of the Pope. The Pope's totalitarian authority was a strong message that resonated with many of the flock.

I learned not to question authority—at home, in school, at church, or in government. Questioning was a punishable offense.

Fortunately, my life experiences and education have allowed me to move past many of these messages in adulthood. I learned about critical thinking from my fellow students and professors at Indiana University. Law school was an education in considering and questioning legal issues from multiple perspectives. There are not necessarily right or wrong answers to legal dilemmas, there being many areas of the law subject to reasonable interpretation. It was acceptable—even encouraged---to consider unpopular or improbable legal positions.

These academic experiences taught me to be less accepting of "pronouncements" from religious, business, and government leaders. The world is not black and white; there are many shades of gray and it is up to me to determine what is true for me.

Trump's political rallies demonstrate that many Americans still value the idea of a "strongman", a white male figure in charge, to impose order, obedience, and uniformity instead of freedom, independence, and individual rights and responsibilities. His simple but clever emotional appeal to the crowds is a throwback to Hitler's ranting addresses in 1930s Germany. He acknowledges their victimization, just as he believes he has been a victim of the establishment and the press. Trump promises to Make America Great Again, if only the crowd will obediently and blindly follow his lead, backward over the cliff and into history.

Trump and his base may be correct that a representative, participatory form of government can sometimes be a difficult and challenging business—not always as efficient as a totalitarian dictator who can "follow his instincts" and make spur of the moment decisions without regard to diverse opinions, the rule of law, individual rights, Constitutional protections, or traditional values. I believe that most Americans, however, consider freedom, values, diversity, the rule of law, and Constitutional protections to be worth the extra effort.

During and after the Trump Presidency, the term "fascism" has regularly re-surfaced in political columns, podcasts, political essays, and cable television newscasts. Personally, I had only a vague and shallow understanding of the term. Mostly, I associated fascism with Hitler and Nazi Germany.

From my perspective, fascism received very little attention after the end of WWII. It was a tyrannical, failed dinosaur of the past, so why is it returning to the American consciousness? What is its meaning in the context of 21st Century America?

Just as all democracies are not exactly alike, fascism has taken on more than one look. *Wikipedia* defines fascism as "a form of far-right, authoritarian ultra-nationalism characterized by dictatorial power, forcible suppression of opposition, and strong regimentation of society and of the economy, which came to prominence in early 20th Century Europe". In other words, a form of government based on fear, control, anger, suppression, and violence. Authoritarian power can be in one person, one elite group, or one controlling political party. By this definition, today's China, North Korea, Iran, Russia,

Belarus, Hungary, Venezuela, Cuba, and a few other nation-states contain fascist elements.

Typically, some or all of the following conditions have been evident in fascist regimes throughout recent history:

- The existence or appearance of economic turmoil or social unrest—perhaps in the aftermath of a major conflict, natural disaster, economic depression, or medical pandemic;
- Presence of an opportunistic, charismatic, egotistical, amoral, psychotic, and ruthless leader;
- A thirst for unlimited power in the leader, without checks or balances in the governmental system;
- A cult-like following of the leader;
- An overpowering, relentless, misleading propaganda machine;
- Ongoing attacks on a free press;
- An official police force of storm troopers such as the Gestapo or KGB, or a semi-official force such as the KKK, able to suppress, torture, or murder the oppressed;
- Unbridled control over the nation's military;
- Elimination or "loading" of a once independent judiciary;
- Allegations of community or social decline from "the good old days";

- Victim mentality among many of the supporters often associated with the fear of losing their power to another racial or ethnic group;
- Ethnic cleansing/racial purity movements, claiming superiority and blaming "others" for their problems;
- Strong border walls to mercilessly keep out the unwanted "riff-raff", and/or "iron curtains" to keep in and control the oppressed citizenry;
- Ruthless elimination or imprisonment of the opposition;
- Militarization of the nation;
- Nationalistic attitudes that disregard the rights of neighbors;
- Idolization of so-called patriotic symbols such as flags, uniforms, military parades, hats, badges, medals, tanks, war planes, bombs, rockets, guns, swastikas;
- An "us versus them" mentality;
- Police brutality aimed at the "others";
- Control over voting systems;
- Voter suppression of minority groups;
- Control over Legislatures and the Judiciary;
- Violence without legal or moral restraints;
- Anti-intellectualism (smart, educated people are inclined to understand what is going on and ask embarrassing questions); and
- Selective versions of history that deny embarrassing or regrettable eras.

If some of these characteristics of fascism sound alarmingly familiar to you in 21st-Century America, you are not alone in your concerns. I am reminded of a saying attributed to Benito Mussolini explaining his successful creation of a fascist regime in Italy: "If you pluck a chicken, one feather at a time, nobody will ever notice that, at some point, the chicken is wholly without feathers."

George Orwell warned us about a fascist future in his classic book, *1984.* Traditional democratic values were suppressed with elimination of free thought, free speech, free assembly, and free press. Those engaged in such activities were "enemies of the people". Big Brother strictly controlled all aspects of society. Communication channels were used only for propaganda purposes. Fear and intolerance were the order of the day, with elimination of all individual human rights. Government-sponsored lies, violence, torture, and terror ran rough-shod over dissenters. It was a society based on deception, fear, intimidation, anger, violence, injustice, and hate—not the kind of society that most Americans look forward to experiencing in their collective future.

I am not predicting a fascist revolution or that Donald J. Trump will be the charismatic and amoral psychopath who will successfully replace our Democracy with a *1984* level of fascism. I am gravely concerned that either Mr. Trump, or a successor wannabe Trump such as a governor from Florida or a Senator from Texas, will jump at the opportunity to continue to exploit and expand Trumpism in America. In order to inherit Trump's angry, misguided base of voters, they will push us in a fascist direction—one feather at a time—until it may be too late to turn back to a government by and for the people.

Fear seems to ignite an anger and hatred that thrives in the minds and hearts of too many Americans. We are living in an American society that has been permeated with polarization, anger, and hate. All it takes is an amoral, ruthless, opportunistic leader to energize that fear and anger for personal and political gain—turning the Collective American Consciousness irreversibly toward the dark side. Twenty-first Century America appears to be all too ripe for the plucking to continue--and possibly to accelerate to a point of no return.

It will be up to the majority of Americans who believe in freedom, the American Constitution, individual rights and responsibilities, equal opportunity and justice for all, integration, tolerance, diversity, the rule of law, and a representative form of government, to move us in that direction. It will require many of us—from diverse backgrounds and experiences--to work together to push the collective consciousness away from divisive fear and hatred, and toward a kinder, gentler, more loving, free, and inclusive United States of America.

As the United States Constitution was being finalized, a bystander asked Benjamin Franklin what type of government the delegates had created. His response, "A Republic, if you can keep it". The ball is now in the peoples' court to keep America's experiment in representative government alive. It is literally a battle for the soul of America.

Part One. The History of Fascism in 20ᵗʰ-Century Europe.

"When fascism came into power, most people were unprepared, both theoretically and practically. They were unable to believe that man could exhibit such propensities for evil, such lust for power, such disregard for the rights of the weak, or such yearning for submission. Only a few had been aware of the rumbling of the volcano preceding the outbreak."
Erich Fromm

In the past, fascism has taken various forms in different cultures and with different leaders. It is not a "one size fits all" political approach. There are some common characteristics, however, that help to define the conditions in which fascism flourishes.

Fearful times of economic and/or social turmoil provide fertile ground for the growth of fascism. Fear, anger, depression, perceived or alleged injustice, widespread poverty of the masses, high unemployment, natural disasters, crime waves, violence, medical pandemics, and racial or social unrest all have the potential to fan the flames of fascism. In such an environment, all that is needed is a charismatic, opportunistic leader in search of power to light the match that burns down the existing order. Such a leader is often willing to use violence and insurrection to achieve his goals.

Governments that are seen as corrupt, weak, dysfunctional, or ineffective add vulnerability to the rise of fascism. It becomes relatively easy to stir up already-angry masses to overthrow such an existing order. Violence and intimidation are often orchestrated by the leader to take control of power, followed by the use of brutal, strong-arm tactics to retain power. With violent elimination of opposing forces, an effective police or military state can do away with a free press, voting rights, legal protections, a "checks and balances" system of government, and an independent judiciary.

There is often a strong anti-intellectual attitude with fascist leaders, knowing that highly educated people are more prone to ask probing questions. This anti-intellectual attitude may sometimes lead to mistrust among the masses of science and medical research. The use of propaganda is a recurring theme with fascist leaders. Critical thinking can be a strong defense against propaganda campaigns. Messages tend to be relatively simple and endlessly repeated. Emotional appeal typically trumps reason, often based on fear, anger, and hatred.

Such propaganda messages as nationalistic excuses for invading neighboring countries, incredulous and illogical conspiracy theories, unfounded allegations of voter fraud, stolen elections, racial superiority/inferiority, micro-chips hidden in vaccines, witch hunts, hoaxes, and border invasions by gangs, do not require evidence—it is enough to have the messages consistently repeated by a dictator, at political rallies, or by party leaders, radical talk show hosts, biased cable news sources, and foreign-sponsored social media to make the propaganda the new reality.

Truth has no place in a propaganda campaign!

Strong, brutal, opportunistic, and charismatic leaders were common characteristics of the two most notable fascist experiments in Europe in the 20th Century. Both Mussolini and Hitler were willing and able to viciously eliminate all opposition in their quests for unlimited power to control the government, and therefore the populous. Legal norms and restraints were largely ignored, as were traditional moral and ethical standards. They created an environment in which long-established "Christian" values became increasingly irrelevant.

Fascism is not to be confused with traditional conservatism. Conservativism tends to want to preserve order and the status quo for the "ins" at the expense of the "outs". It is the age-old concept of "I've got mine. Everyone else is on their own." Capitalism is a key component of conservative thought. Using the existing democratic, capitalistic system, conservatism tends to result in significant wealth gaps within society and only minimal safety nets for the poor.

Neither is fascism to be confused with liberalism, which is usually an attempt to work within the existing governmental system, but tax the rich at a higher rate in order to spread the wealth more evenly among the middle class and the poor. Typically, strong safety nets are available to the people in the form of social security benefits, welfare payments, universal or affordable healthcare, a strong and affordable public school system from pre-K through college, government-subsidized childcare, family leave arrangements, affordable housing, labor protections, a justice and law enforcement system that is intended to be fair to everyone, regulation of industry and banking, consumer protections, equal opportunities, environmental concerns, and a collective consciousness of fairness and sharing.

Both conservatives and liberals tend to work within the system, but try to push the envelope in their preferred direction. Although far from perfect, in America this system has worked for centuries to maintain a relatively balanced, stable, representative form of government. Conservatives and liberals have both survived and thrived in America, sometimes even working together for the common good of the Nation.

In sharp contrast, fascism intends to destroy the old order in favor of a new order—an order in which the state's (i.e. the dictator's) interests take precedence over individual rights. Fascist supporters tend to admire physical strength, brutality, a strong nation-state with a strong leader to blindly follow.

Although there were aspects of fascism in other European countries in the 20th Century, such as Stalin's Russia and Franco's Spain, the most striking fascist models evolved in 1920s Italy and 1930s Germany.

Mussolini in Italy.

Benito Mussolini has been credited with developing the ideological basis for fascism, promoting the state as the ultimate end and the people's interests as secondary. An avowed racist, he believed in a hierarchy of races. It was Mussolini's belief that the stronger races were justified in subjugating and dominating inferior races.

Mussolini considered Italians, descendants of the Roman Empire, to be a superior race. Slavs and dark-skinned people were considered to be inferior races. In his mind, the Italian nation had the right to expand into territories controlled by the inferior races—not unlike the "Manifest Destiny" philosophy of taking Indian lands from an inferior race for the benefit of the superior European-descended white settlers, in 19th-Century America. Mussolini did not begin his political life as a fascist or an autocrat. He was an early advocate of socialism, working his way into a leadership position with the Italian Socialist party. His early intentions apparently were to improve the lot of the Italian people.

Following the ravages of WWI, much of Europe was struggling to recover socially and economically. There were no "winners" in WWI. Italy, one of the victorious casualties of the War, contained segments of the population that were strongly nationalistic.

The Italian government was widely perceived as weak, corrupt, and incompetent, providing an opening for a strong leader. Mussolini was only too willing to step into the breach. Having started out as a revolutionary socialist, by the end of WWI he considered the concept of socialism dead. He saw the need for a dictator who could make a "clean sweep" to confront Italy's problems.

Mussolini quickly moved in the political direction of nationalism and authoritarianism. The more power he acquired, the stronger was his need for more. He had a "rabble-rousing" ability to spread discord among the impoverished masses. In the civil turmoil following WWI, he brought together several fascist groups in Italy that became the Partito Nationale Fascistas.

Through brutal violence and vicious propaganda, this fascist party gained control over the inept Italian government. His supporters all wore black shirts at his political rallies, and were inspired by his rhetoric to round up, beat, even kill socialists and communists. Mussolini encouraged and inspired this mob violence, and soon took control over the mobs.

The Italian government did little to combat the lawlessness of the fascists and their black-shirted violence. Musolini's daring, high-stakes "March on Rome" was surprisingly uncontested by the ruling government, and in 1922, at the age of 38, Benito Mussolini was invited by King Victor Emmanuel, III, to become the Prime Minister of Italy.

Paranoid by nature, Mussolini suspected parliament was anti-fascist, and quickly took away their powers. Anyone even suspected of being anti-fascist was arrested and imprisoned without the need for a trial.

Once in power in the 1920s, Mussolini developed a strong cult following. An excellent writer and orator, he gained and maintained complete control over the Italian government. Many Italians welcomed his dictatorial authority.

Mussolini made political deals with the Catholic Church to keep its power over the Catholic population in check. The Lateran Pact of 1929 established a separate Vatican City and was his effort to rein in the power of the Pope over the Italian people. Other political parties were eliminated and Mussolini's party obtained monopolistic powers with "El Duce" in firm command. The rare elections were in the nature of plebiscites with only yes or no choices. The Italian Parliament was essentially powerless after 1922.

In 1925 Mussolini declared himself to be the dictator of Italy. He demanded unlimited powers to control elections, allowing him to rig them in the Fascist Party's favor. All Communist members of Parliament were arrested, and Socialists were expelled from Parliament. The Fascist Party controlled political speeches, movies, news reels, radio stations, books, magazines, and newspapers, creating a massive and monopolistic propaganda machine. Diverse points of view were buried in Mussolini's Italy.

Hitler was well aware of Mussolini's political successes in Italy. In the 1930s, an admiring Hitler connected with Mussolini, and they joined forces to become partners in crime. In 1936 Nazi Germany and Fascist Italy signed a treaty of cooperation, and the Rome/Berlin Axis was officially in business.

Like Hitler, Mussolini initially improved economic conditions in his country. Public works were initiated, industry was modernized, and improvements were made in the area of agriculture. The infrastructure of the country was updated, with new roads, aqueducts, railroad tracks, and trains began running somewhat on schedule. He was highly acclaimed as a political genius by some foreign observers—including American politicians. Like Hitler, Mussolini quickly turned his attention in the direction of military armaments and nationalistic expansion plans. He grew the military, and tried (somewhat unsuccessfully) to build an armaments industry to support his military ambitions. Mussolini's foreign policy goal was to restore the grandeur of the Roman Empire by expansion of Italy's territorial conquests.

El Duce ordered the Italian military to intervene in the Spanish Civil War in 1936, backing Francisco

Franco in his fight against communist and socialist factions. It was also a practical way to gain valuable fighting experience for his military and their new weapons.

Mussolini brutally invaded Ethiopia, with the intention of creating a colonial empire fashioned after England and France. In 1939 Italy invaded and annexed Albania. His aggressive expansion efforts ignited national pride in many of the Italian people. When WWII began later that year, Mussolini and Italy joined with Hitler, and came down on the side of Germany.

Interestingly, an insecure Mussolini discouraged his "advisors" from proposing ideas that might cause him to doubt his instincts, which he "knew were always right". Like former President Trump, he surrounded himself with sycophants and toadies who bowed to his personal brilliance. Not surprisingly, the absence of strong, independent-minded leadership around him eventually led to his downfall.

WWII was the beginning of the end for Mussolini, as significant portions of the Italian people were not enthralled with their subservient war-marriage to Germany. As Italy's military defeats from the Allies mounted, Mussolini was forcibly removed from power and imprisoned in 1943.

German paratroopers rescued Mussolini from captivity in 1944, and Hitler installed him as a puppet-dictator over portions of Northern Italy still being defended by Germany against the advancing Allies. The total capitulation of Italy to the Allies late in the War led to Mussolini's violent death at the hands of an angry mob and a firing squad.

Fascism died in Italy with the death of its fallen dictator.

Hitler in Germany.

Post-WWI Germany was a chaotic and miserable place to live. Millions of German soldiers had been killed in battle; the flu pandemic of 1918 had killed many more; the victorious nations were extorting reparations from an already bankrupt German economy; inflation was running rampant, and leadership was in dismal disarray.

German citizens were embarrassed by their unexpected military defeat and blamed German government leaders. The Versailles Treaty dictated that Germany accept total blame for the War and totally disarm. Vital German territories and natural resources were ceded to the victors. Turmoil, sickness, hunger, unemployment, misery, anger, and shame were the prevailing winds of Post-War Germany.

It was in the midst of this social and economic unrest that Adolph Hitler, a German corporal in WWI, made his move. The weakness and political instability of the Weimar Republic contributed to the rise of multiple political groups, including the German Workers Party. Hitler became the head of this party in 1920 and renamed it the National Socialist Workers (Nazi) Party.

The Nazi party quickly became a force for promoting Germany and the German race. It was nationalistic, in favor of re-taking ceded territories, expanding Germany's borders, and tapped into the age-old German bias against Jews. The Nazi party was strongly antisemitic from the very beginning.

Similar to Mussolini's rise in Italy, the German people were looking for someone (anyone) to lead them out of their miserable conditions.

Already delusional, Hitler initially overestimating his self-importance. He took foolish political risks to seize political control of the Bavarian State. His Munich Beer Hall Putsch failed, leading to prison time for Hitler.

Hitler used his time in prison to write Mein Kampf, an autobiographical manifesto which explained his personal struggle, political philosophy, and future plans for Germany. Mein Kampf became a roadmap of his intentions and was required reading for his followers. It foretold his vision of the "master race" and the bloody elimination of the Jews. Mein Kampf appealed to many dissatisfied white supremacist elements in Germany.

When Hitler was released from prison in 1925, he quickly re-established himself as a shrewd and powerful political force in Germany.

Exploiting the election system with an aggressive onslaught of Nazi Party violence and propaganda, Hitler manipulated the inept political machinery to become Chancellor in January, 1933. Against the better judgment of established leaders in Germany, his deceptive assurances persuaded the existing powers to give Hitler a chance—fully expecting him to fail.

Hitler immediately set out to dismantle the Weimar Republic. Losing no time, the supportive German Reichstag passed the Enabling Act in March, 1933 which allowed Hitler to enact laws without the approval of Parliament or President von Hindenburg. He then banned all other political parties and consolidated his power as dictator, using his political secret police force (the Gestapo) to squelch all opposition.

This opportunistic grab of political power from the establishment was quick and brutal. The military, government officials, and German citizens were required to pledge personal loyalty to Hitler— another action much admired by Donald Trump nearly a century later.

Young "pure" Germans were enlisted in programs of indoctrination into Nazi philosophy, forming a generation of Hitler Youth who were supposed to represent the future of the super race. Swearing complete loyalty to Hitler, they also served as a ready source of informants on their parents, grandparents, and other family members who might have reservations about Hitler and his fascist policies.

As the authoritarian dictator, Hitler went about creating a pure German race, ruthlessly eliminating the "undesirables" such as Jews, Gypsies, homosexuals, intellectuals, the disabled, and any other minorities who did not measure up to the master race. They were initially humiliated, isolated, and excluded from participation in business and society. In phase 2, they were subsequently rounded up for slave labor and extermination camps.

Over six million of these "undesirables" were killed by Hitler and his cronies. Many "good Germans" contracted a strong sense of denial, choosing to turn a blind eye to the systematic persecution and murder of their fellow countrymen.

Under Hitler, the German armament industry came to life at an astonishing speed in direct violation of the Versailles Treaty. Initial efforts were done in secret, but Hitler's 1935 announcement that he would rearm Germany caused shockwaves around the world. There were widespread voices of condemnation, but no action to interrupt his plans. In effect, Hitler thumbed his nose at the victors of WWI, and the victors shrugged their shoulders and wrung their hands in despair.

Plans were disclosed to build an air force, reinstitute conscription, and create an army. By the late 1930s, Germany was illegally producing vast numbers of warplanes, tanks, guns, submarines, and battleships. The army and navy were expanding exponentially as the rest of the world looked on with alarm. Due in large part to the military buildup, Hitler had performed an economic miracle with the German economy. Unemployment rapidly disappeared. The German army grew to about a million soldiers, the arms industry further reduced unemployment in Germany, and support for the Nazi Party continued to grow.

In 1938 Germany annexed Austria and then the Sudetenland. Appeased and unchecked in 1939, Hitler recklessly and boldly continued his expansionist plans into Czechoslovakia. Further emboldened by a lack of international reaction, he then invaded Poland, leading Britain and France to finally declare war on Germany. WWII had begun. Anyone in Germany opposed to Hitler's plans were suppressed or eliminated. Individual rights were subordinate to national interests.

Unlimited power can have an intoxicating effect. Surrounded by toadies and sycophants, delusional fascist leaders often over-estimate their own intelligence and instincts. Throughout the conduct of WWII, Hitler consistently chose to follow his instincts rather than the guidance of his military leaders. Eventually, his instincts bordered on insanity and led to German military defeats and the ultimate demise of the Third Reich in 1945.

Hitler did not ask for a re-count, or claim the war was stolen from him. He simply chose suicide rather than accepting defeat, and managed to bring the German nation plummeting down with him— another failed experiment in fascism.

Part Two. The Faces of Fascism in 21st-Century America.

"When fascism comes to America, it will be wrapped in the flag and carrying a cross." Sinclair Lewis

In my view, it is unlikely that fascism, if or when it takes control of America's future, will happen suddenly as one event or revolution. Rather it will be an evolutionary process: "a creeping fascism" or "plucking the chicken". Many fear we are already well along the path of fascism. What might a totalitarian, fascist state in America look like?

It might be useful to look at the psychological patterns of both 20th-Century's and 21st-Century's most notorious fascist dictators around the world in order to better recognize the potential emergence of an American dictator and a fascist state.

An authoritarian dictatorship can be defined as a form of government in which a single person or a single party has absolute power.

The Psychological Patterns of 20th-Century Dictators Continue to Prevail with Many 21st-Century Dictators.

According to U.S. Intelligence sources in the 1930s and 1940s, Adolph Hitler shared many of the personality traits that some of us now identify with former President Trump. Hitler considered himself to be an authority on every subject; was unable to admit a mistake; was above the law; never accepted responsibility for his actions if they failed; took credit for things that went right; blamed his "enemies" for anything that went wrong; thought that people would believe big lies easier than little ones; and that any lie, repeated often enough, would eventually be believed.

Based on observations from a distance, Hitler was diagnosed by various psychologists and psychiatrists as having narcissistic personality disorder, possibly bipolar, schizophrenic, anti-social, and a psychopath who was delusional and out of touch with reality. Adolph Hitler remains the role model for a psychopathic, unbalanced, delusional and dangerous autocrat.

Benito Mussolini considered fascism to be a religion. He has been described as narcissistic, racist, arrogant, and xenophobic. He was the charismatic leader, and his followers were like a religious cult. Like Hitler and Trump, he considered himself to be an authority on every subject. Diverse, independent views were discouraged and ignored in Mussolini's circle.

Joseph Stalin was physically and psychologically abused by an alcoholic father in his youth, while his mother was emotionally distant and aloof. As a possible result, Stalin grew up as an aggressive, angry, cruel, sadistic, and ruthless bully. He was insecure and trusted no one, routinely purging his group of closest supporters. He demanded absolute personal loyalty, and no one was safe from his vicious purges.

During the Trump Era, America got a taste of what it might be like to have an autocratic psychopath in control of the levers of government. Before, during, and after his four years in Office, Trump exhibited socially irresponsible behavior. His alleged corrupt business practices, reported and admitted sexual abuse of women, racism, xenophobia, and egotistical attitudes were well documented before he ran for election as President of the United States.

Focused only on his own wants and needs, Trump easily disregards the rights of others. With an inability to distinguish between right and wrong, he was and is willing to lie without remorse. A delusional manipulator of "facts" to fit his needs, he clearly considers himself above the law.

The American system of democratic checks and balances restrained Trump from going completely over the edge during his term as President. With Vladimir Putin's Russian invasion of Ukraine, the world received a clear picture of a full-blown psychopath in absolute control of a nation and its huge military, with a stockpile of chemical and nuclear weapons at his disposal. Trump admittedly admires Putin as smart, shrewd, and a genius for invading Ukraine.

A modern-day dictator, Vladimir Putin can be described as psychopathic, narcissistic, anti-social, paranoid, manipulative, dominating, controlling, aggressive, ambitious, cruel, unable to distinguish between right and wrong, a brutal suppressor of opposition, a risk-taker, and totally void of empathy. He is rarely described as warm, lovable, or caring about anyone but himself. Putin is the nightmare version of what an American fascist leader might look like. Russia is rapidly returning to a nightmare version of what a totalitarian, fascist American state would look like.

One of Putin's most trusted allies, Alexander Lukashenko of Belarus, has tenaciously held on to power through rigged elections for nearly thirty years. His brutal pattern of silencing dissent, routinely jailing and torturing his critics—including journalists--will be his lasting legacy.

Hungary's Victor Orban has effectively dismantled the democratic foundation of a previously democratic Country. He has found a way to manipulate the system to control the opposition, using government-controlled propaganda to silence pro-democracy forces within Hungary. Spreading xenophobic fear of immigrants—Muslims in particular—he touts his regime as the only thing preventing a Muslim takeover of the Country. He has wrapped himself in the cloak of white Christianity, and considers multiculturism and diversity of viewpoints as threats to his vision of Hungary.

Orban is a popular favorite of some conservative voices in America, including Steve Bannon and Tucker Carlson. Bannon and Carlson eagerly participate in Orban's propaganda machine. They admire this mostly-white, Christian nation fending off the Muslim refugees. To be fair, Tucker Carlson eagerly participates in Putin's propaganda machine as well.

Hungary is an example of how a once democratic country can slowly sink into the morass of an autocratic, fascist state—all in the name of Christianity. This chicken has been plucked, one feather at a time, transforming the nation from democracy to autocracy.

Bashar al-Assad has ruled Syria with an iron fist for more than two decades. His father, Hafez al-Assad, preceded him as dictator of Syria for three decades, making Syria an autocratic family operation for more than half a century. The regime has become more and more dependent on Vladimir Putin to remain in power.

Pro-democracy uprisings in Syria in 2011 were brutally suppressed by al-Assad's security forces, resulting in a full-blown civil war. His use of illegal chemical weapons against the opposition brought international disgrace on the regime. The Russian military has propped up the regime in the face of international opposition.

Ali Khamenei is the supreme leader of Iran. According to *Wikipedia*, he has been in power for more than four decades. The military, judiciary, and state television are all under the control of the supreme leader. He makes the final decisions on the economy, foreign policy, religion, and all other aspects of governing the theocracy of Iran.

Khamenei is considered "inviolable"—sort of like the Pope is "infallible"—and Iranians who question him or insult him are severely punished.

Kim Jung-un succeeded his father, Kim Jong-il, as supreme leader of North Korea in 2011. Before them, Kim Jong-il's father, had been dictator since

1948. This ruling family has served as head of the Workers Party of Korea, the ruling party of North Korea, since its formation in 1948. It operates as a family business with an enslaved workforce.

The government closely supervises the lives of the North Korean citizens, severely limiting freedom of expression. The military is the intimidating focus of activity. The daily lives of common workers in North Korea involve suppression, forced labor, and near-starvation.

Donald Trump has a particular fondness for Kim Jung-un, having exchanged "love letters" with him following their unproductive diplomatic summit meetings.

The prevailing themes of these autocrats include narcissism, egotism, psychopathic tendencies, cruelty, lack of empathy, nationalistic attitudes, emphasis on militarization, propaganda machines, suppression of opposition, control over the ballot box, dominance over legislatures and judiciaries, strong-arm tactics by law enforcement, disregard for due process or individual rights, and family dynasties.

Reminiscent of attitudes of many Republican members of Congress in the 1930s who publicly admired what Benito Mussolini and Adolph Hitler were doing in Europe, former President Trump readily acknowledges that he better identifies with this cast of strong-men than he relates to the democratically-elected leaders of America's allies in Western Europe. Authoritarian rule is in his DNA, and he has spread this disease to many of his political followers.

Trumpism will probably remain a threat to American democracy long after Donald Trump passes from the political scene.

One-Party Control of the Election Process.

With the important exceptions of Jim Crowe voter suppression practices in some Southern states, and denial of women's right to vote before 1920, America has a long tradition of a bi-partisan election system that guarantees free and fair elections. It is a system that has been modeled and admired throughout the Free World, based on bi-partisan and independent poll workers and vote counters. A checks and balances system maintains the integrity of the electoral process.

There have been relatively few pockets of corrupt or unfair national elections in U.S. history. The bi-partisan system has worked for a long time in America.

Political control over the strings of American government have gone back and forth over the decades. For more than two centuries, Republicans and Democrats alike have accepted the results of national elections—until Donald J. Trump's shocking rejection and attempted overthrow of the democratic process following the 2020 Presidential Election.

Following Trump's unwillingness to concede the 2020 Presidential Election to Joe Biden, and a failed violent attempt at Insurrection attributed to his unfounded allegations that the election was stolen from him, Trump loyalists activated Plan B to destroy the independent, bi-partisan election process and replace it with one-party control of who gets to vote and determine how the votes get counted.

Republican-controlled state legislatures quickly took up Trump's cause, enacting voter suppression laws that will make it more difficult for minority voters to participate in future elections. Redistricting efforts were re-designed for one-party control of Congress and state legislatures.

Equally troubling, long-time poll workers and impartial election officials became the victims of intimidation and death threats after the 2020 election. Many of these independent workers, who had maintained the integrity of the election process for decades, were forced out of office or resigned to protect the personal safety of themselves and their families. GOP governors and legislatures then proceeded to fill the vacuum with partisan election officials who could be counted on to "do the right thing" for their party in future elections.

Proposed state laws have even gone so far as to empower the state legislatures who disagree with the vote of the people to designate a different political slate of Electors to vote when the Electoral College convenes to formally cast the State's votes for the new President and Vice President.

One-party control of the election process is a giant step down the slippery slope of fascism, and strong forces are currently at work to accomplish this step along the path.

A President Above the Law.

A June 1972 break-in at the Democratic National Committee headquarters led to the arrest of burglars with political connections to President Nixon's re-election campaign (CREEP). They were caught wire-tapping phones and stealing documents. Nixon denied any knowledge and took aggressive steps to cover up his involvement.

President Nixon and his aides planned to have the CIA impede the FBI's investigation into the break-in. Washington Post reporters Bob Woodward and Carl Bernstein began uncovering damaging evidence against Nixon. As President, Nixon desperately attempted to obstruct justice in the face of Senate investigations, Supreme Court decisions, and demands from Special Prosecutor Archibald Cox—an eventual victim of the famous "Saturday Night Massacre."

When Cox issued a subpoena to Nixon for tapes of conversations in the Oval Office, President Nixon refused to honor the subpoena. He then ordered Attorney General Elliott Richardson to fire Special Prosecutor Cox, but Richardson refused and resigned instead. Nixon then ordered Deputy Attorney General William Ruckelshaus to fire Cox, and he also refused and resigned. The impeachment process began ten days later.

Congress was infuriated by this gross abuse of presidential power. The House Judiciary Committee voted to impeach Nixon for obstruction of justice, abuse of power, criminal cover-up, and violation of the Constitution. The Senate was prepared to convict the President.

When Richard Nixon attempted to place himself above the law in the 1970s, his own Republican party refused to allow him to do so. He was forced to comply with Congressional investigators and their subpoenas. Faced with conviction for impeachment by an independent Senate, he resigned in disgrace. Republican members of the House and Senate understood their Constitutional responsibilities, and refused to allow Nixon to defy the rule of law, Congress, the Judiciary, and the Constitution.

Fast-forward to the Trump Era, with starkly similar impeachable offenses. Too many Republican members of Congress have been in sheepish lock-step with their dear leader. They have willingly acceded their Congressional powers in order to protect themselves in upcoming primary elections. They are afraid of Trump's voter base. Some of them have shamelessly jumped on Trump's bandwagon while holding their noses at his actions.

Many Republican politicians may privately abhor Trump and his tactics, but they fear Trump's political power to endorse his hand-picked loyal candidates in future primaries, thereby ousting any disloyal (to Trump) members of the current "in" crowd. The very few Republican politicians who have chosen to publicly defy Trump have been shunned and censured by their Republican colleagues, and most have opted to announce their retirements rather than stand for re-election in such a toxic atmosphere.

The political power that Trump has amassed, and continues to abuse, is making a mockery of the Legislative Branch of Government.

The hotly contested investigation into the violent January 6th Insurrection is ongoing, and the legal force of Congressional subpoenas in the Post-Trump Era remains an ongoing mystery. Contempt of Congress may be an empty gesture in the future. It is yet unknown whether Trump's "loading" of the Federal Judiciary will protect him and his cohorts from being responsible for their participation in the "big lie" and the violent Insurrection.

The obvious trend in American politics is to concentrate more and more power in the Administrative Branch. Congress is becoming more and more partisan, and less and less relevant to the governing process.

The table has been set for Trump or another authoritarian personality to grab absolute power!

A Loaded Federal Judiciary.

Before giving up its legislative power, during the Obama Administration, the Republican-controlled Senate used its majority status to block President Obama's Supreme Court nominee, Merrick Garland, from even getting a hearing. The Majority Leader merely sat on the nomination for nearly a year until after Trump's election as President. This was an unprecedented abuse of Congressional power that led to nomination and confirmation of three right-wing Supreme Court Justices nominated by Trump, upsetting the balance of the Court.

In addition, the Republican-controlled Senate during the Trump Era did little else but load the entire Federal Judiciary with Trump's far-right nominees.

Following the 2020 National Election, and despite opinions from his own Attorney General and Homeland Security that no serious fraud occurred, Trump waged a vicious battle to overturn Biden's victory.

Trump and his allies filed 62 election lawsuits in state and federal courts seeking to overturn the election. Many cases were summarily dismissed by the courts for lack of standing or for lack of evidence. State Supreme Courts in Arizona and Nevada declined to hear Trump's appeals. Pennsylvania and Michigan Supreme Courts denied the lawsuits brought to their courts on appeal. Federal judges all over the country dismissed lawsuits filed by allies of the Trump campaign.

To its credit, Federal Courts—including the United States Supreme Court—did not buy into Trump's unfounded allegations that the 2020 election was stolen from him. Trump was rebuffed in multiple Federal Courts, including the Supreme Court. The extent to which this was due to lack of evidence, the ineptness of Trump's legal team, or to unbiased judges, may never be fully known.

With the current imbalance on the bench of SCOTUS, there are fresh signs that long-held Constitutional protections are in jeopardy. Individual rights and protections are taking a back pew to religious dogma. This is a dangerous trend in the direction of fascism.

Employment of the Military to Aid in a Political Coup.

Coups d'etats have not been uncommon in many parts of the world. Rather than going through a bloody civil war, plotters instead overthrow the existing governmental apparatus and seize control of the country. Often, the nation's military is used to back up a coup—either directly or as a support for the plotters. Nations subject to coups tend to be small and underdeveloped. The larger and more developed the nation, the less likelihood of an internal coup.

The U.S. Constitution and long-standing political traditions have so far protected the American system from suffering a political coup. Democratic traditions, civilian control of the military, and a system for the orderly transfer of power have made political coups unlikely in America. That said, the January 6th Insurrection was a violent attempt to overthrow the will of the people and interrupt the peaceful transfer of power from the Trump Administration to the Biden Administration. By definition, it was an unsuccessful political coup attempt.

Referring to "my generals", Trump seemed to be genuinely surprised to learn that the U.S. Military understood their obligation to be apolitical, and refused to be a part of his coup attempt. The Joint Chiefs of Staff and top military officers successfully resisted efforts by Trump to use the U.S. Military to be involved in his political ambitions, including seizing voting machines and ballots, and the suppression of peaceful demonstrations by American citizens. It was not for Trump's lack of trying.

Trump tested the boundaries between civilian and military relations by urging that active-duty troops be utilized to violently suppress peaceful Black Lives Matter protests. Chairman of the Joint Chiefs, General Millie, was lured into appearing next to Trump as the National Guard took violent action to dispel demonstrators near the White House, so that

Trump could have a photo op with a Bible in front of a nearby church.

Former Chairman of the Joint Chiefs of Staff, General Martin Dempsey, protested on Twitter Trump's efforts to enlist the military for political purposes: "America is not a battleground. Our fellow citizens are not the enemy." Admiral Mike Mullen wrote in The Atlantic: "Whatever Trump's goal in conducting his visit, he laid bare his disdain for the rights of peaceful protest in this country, gave succor to the leaders of other countries who take comfort in our domestic strife, and risked further politicizing the men and women of the armed forces."

Trump actively explored the options of using military force and law enforcement to patrol the polls, interfere with the election process, seize the voting machines, and stop officials from counting the ballots. It is difficult to imagine a more intimidating atmosphere for a free and fair election process.

General Millie, Chairman of the Joint Chiefs, was so concerned about Trump's inappropriate use of the military for political purposes that he took the unusual step to remind all branches of the military to resist potential orders from Trump to attack civilians following the 2020 election. But for some courageous, patriotic military leaders, Trump may have successfully taken over the U.S. Military to help him stage his coup.

Once in control of the military, it would not be an easy task to wrest control away from an autocratic leader.

Encouragement of Police Brutality Against the Opposition.

At Trump's political rallies before, during, and after his term in office, the mood has often bordered on violence. He encourages chants such as "lock her up" in reference to Hillary Clinton, his opponent in the 2016 election. He suggested the same fate for his predecessors in office. Constitutionally guaranteed due process protections were totally missing from Trump's rhetoric.

Trump has encouraged attendees at his rallies to "knock the crap out of hecklers" while blaming his political opponents for violence at his events. He has offered to pay legal fees for any of his followers who are arrested for violence against his opponents. Trump actually applauded Filipino President Rodrigo Duterte for his policy of encouraging police and vigilante mobs to murder over 6,000 "suspected" drug dealers without any form of due process. It demonstrated an unbridled admiration for autocratic leadership. He freely admits that he feels more comfortable around the autocratic leaders of Russia, China, North Korea, Turkey, Belarus, and Hungary compared with his strained relationships with the democratically-elected leaders of America's traditional allies in Western Europe.

Openly advocating police brutality, Trump has exacerbated the problem with his rhetoric. As he encourages governors to "dominate" peaceful Black Lives Matter protestors and threatens to send in the military, he has consistently made race relations worse. Trump has even promoted vigilante justice—echoes of KKK "justice" of the past.

In reaction to police removing disruptive demonstrators at his rallies, Trump has encouraged the police to "please don't be too nice" in their treatment of the demonstrators. He has made frequent comments promoting torture of his "enemies". He applauded harsh law enforcement treatment of protesters and journalists. He described police violence against reporters as "actually a beautiful sight".

Some of the Trump base were only too willing to carry out his instructions, taking violent actions against anyone in opposition to their leader. Vigilante justice and armed intimidation were the results of his conduct. The January 6th Insurrection was simply the culmination of more than four years of these messages of violence.

Much of the police brutality has been aimed at people of color. This is just one more indication of the re-birth of fascism in America.

Attacks on the Free Press.

The First Amendment to the U.S. Constitution protects a free press. The Founding Fathers were well aware of the importance of the freedom to question the government and express adverse opinions.

Authoritarian regimes universally stifle the press. Autocrats have little tolerance for criticism from an independent source. Journalists are being rounded up, imprisoned, tortured, and murdered around the globe. China, Russia, North Korea, Belarus, Iran, Saudi Arabia, Venezuela, Nicaragua, and Myanmar are recent examples of violent attacks on a free and independent press. Putin is in the process of "purging" all remnants of a free press in Russia.

Totalitarian regimes have become more and more intimidating in their actions against the press, arresting, imprisoning, and sometimes murdering journalists. Censorship and seizure of phone records do not bode well for the future of a free and independent press in many parts of the globe—including America.

According to the American Civil Liberties Union, a protector of Constitutional rights, Trump is no friend of freedom of the press. He has threatened to "open up our libel laws" to make it easier to sue journalists who do not agree with him and his behavior, referring to journalists as "scum" and "slime." He blacklisted reporters and news sources from campaign events. In true fascist style, he threatened to cancel the broadcast licenses of media that covered him in a negative way.

Trump regularly refers to members of the press as "enemies of the people" unless they join his propaganda machine. A few far-right institutions, such as Fox News, Breitbart, and some talk show hosts are exempted from the term, as they are part of his propaganda blitz. Any news coverage adverse to Trump is referred to as "fake news". His terms and attitude toward the free press are lifted right out of George Orwell's *1984,* and further legitimize attacks on the press by other autocrats around the Globe.

The more authoritarian the regime, the less tolerance there is for criticism. Many of the increasing numbers of attacks on journalists in the United States have been from law enforcement officials—sometimes deliberately targeted by the police.

Truth has been increasingly under attack in the United States during the Trump Era.

Integration of Church and State.

Theocracies are not uncommon in the history of the world, including Rome, Egypt, Israel, Japan, China, and Tibet. Even today, theocratic governments rule in Vatican City, Yemen, Sudan, Saudi Arabia, Iran, Mauritania, and Afghanistan. It is a form of government in which religious leaders rule based on their uncompromising and often unkind religious dogma. Rulers are considered to be intermediaries receiving divine guidance, and therefore they are not subject to question by the people. Like the infallible Pope, leaders of Theocracies are not to be questioned. Theocracies are the opposite of democracies.

Many early settlers of America came to our shores to escape the religious prosecution and persecution prevalent in many areas of 17th century and 18th century Europe. They yearned to be free to pursue their own religious beliefs—or not. It was no accident that the United States Constitution provided for the separation of church and state.

The Founding Fathers came from a myriad of religious beliefs and non-beliefs. George Washington, Thomas Jefferson, Benjamin Franklin, James Madison and James Monroe did not consider themselves to be "Christians", but rather believed in Deism, a philosophy of human reason to deal with social and political issues.

Their experiences and beliefs formed the foundation for the First Amendment to the Constitution: "Congress shall make no law respecting an establishment of religion, or prohibiting the free exercise thereof." This Amendment became the basis for similar laws in every State of the Union. There was near-universal acceptance of the concept that church and state should remain separate.

In 1947 the U.S. Supreme Court in Everson v. Board of Education ruled that: "no tax, in any amount, large or small, can be levied to support any religious activities or institutions, whatever they may be called, or whatever form they may adopt to teach or practice religion." The wall of separation between church and state must be kept "high and impregnable".

Since 1947, a series of holes have been punched into this wall. In Lemon v. Kurtman, the Supreme Court established the "Lemon Test" to public funding of religious endeavors. The test: 1. The statute must have a secular legislative purpose; 2. Its principal or primary effect cannot enhance or inhibit religion; and 3. The statute must not foster an excessive governmental entanglement with religion.

In 1983 the Court, in Mueller v. Allen, created a "Neutrality Test" to judge state payments to religious schools. The Court held that Minnesota parents could deduct religious school tuition and textbooks regardless of the type of school they attended. The statute was blind to the type of school, although in reality 90% of applicable schools were religious.

The Religious Freedom Restoration Act of 1993 prohibits any federal or state agency from substantially burdening a person's exercise of religion, no matter the person's religious beliefs.

In 2000, the Court in Mitchell v. Helms rejected the long-standing establishment clause. Justice Clarence Thomas wrote the majority opinion that found it constitutionally permissible for Louisiana to use federal grants to purchase educational materials for religious schools. In effect, it became acceptable to divert federal resources to religious purposes.

The conservative majority of the Supreme Court now appears willing to completely lift this prohibition, effectively dismantling the wall between church and state. Since 2000, there have been numerous instances in which federal and state monies have flowed into the coffers of religious schools, churches, and institutions. As a result, there has developed a pattern of efforts by religious groups to gain control of governmental functions.

Along with the financial entanglements, the influence of religion in politics is growing exponentially in America.

Suppression of Freedom of Assembly.

The right to peacefully assemble or to protest is a fundamental right under the First Amendment. This right exists even under conditions when most citizens consider the protest offensive. The Civil Rights Movement would not have gained traction without this important protection. Ironically, this same basic freedom that protects Black Lives Matter protestors also protects KKK marchers who take to the streets to espouse their racist beliefs. The government may not interfere with the peaceful expression of unpopular views. Unless there is real danger of imminent harm or threat to public safety, such rights must be protected.

Unlike in Russia, China, or Iran, public demonstrations and protests have been a cherished tradition in America for centuries. Their frequency and intensity have increased dramatically during the Trump Era, and have not gone over well with former President Trump. He has forcefully pushed back on the rights of peaceful protestors. Protests involving Trump, his policies and practices, have included:

- Demonstrators gathered in cities and towns all over America to protest Trump's harsh anti-immigration policies. Families Belong Together marched to protest Trump's policy of separating children from their parents at the Mexican border. Outside the White House, loudspeakers blasted a recording of babies and children crying. Protesters marched past the Trump International Hotel chanting "shame!". Celebrities and politicians joined together to denounce Trump's "zero tolerance" policy. Demonstrators congregated around Trump golf clubs and other properties;
- Trump pushed back hard against racial justice protests across the country. There were numerous and wide-spread demonstrations in support of Black Lives Matter following the brutal killing of George Floyd—and others--by policemen defended by Trump. His attacks on Critical Race Theory have enraged many in the Black Lives Movement;

- Regular protests at Trump political rallies often lead to violent confrontations between Trump supporters and demonstrators;
- The Women's March was a global event the day after Donald Trump was inaugurated. It was the largest single-day protest in the history of the United States. The goal was to send Trump a message that women's rights are human rights. The Washington March drew over 470,000 people with over 7,000,000 participating world-wide. It was the first of many marches by women to protest Trump's stance on myriad issues, including abortion, immigration, and climate change; and
- Literally thousands of protests and demonstrations have taken place in the United States and elsewhere as a result of Trump's activities.

Many of the gatherings were peaceful, or at least started out peaceful until Trump supporters or law enforcement confronted the protestors. There have been many instances in which Trump has urged his supporters to violence, or encouraged law enforcement to "not be too nice" when arresting demonstrators.

The Unite the Right rally in Charlottesville, Virginia was a white supremacy protest over the removal of a statue of Confederate General Robert E. Lee. Rally attendees and counter protestors clashed, and a neo-nazi fanatic rammed his car into a crowd of counter protestors, killing one and injuring thirty-two others. Trump famously defended these white supremacists as "fine people". He had a far less favorable opinion of the demonstrators at Black Lives Matter rallies. It was fair game for his supporters to protest; protestors against his policies or political stances deserved to be locked up.

Protestors were tear-gassed near the White House in June, 2020, as the police and National Guard cleared Lafayette Park for Trump's photo op holding a bible with General Millie at his side. Days later, General Millie, Chairman of the Joint Chiefs of Staff, apologized and acknowledged that he should not have been present. It gave the perception that the military was involved in domestic politics, which was clearly Trump's intent by urging General Millie to be at his side.

Former Defense Secretary James Mattis said Trump's involvement of military officials in the situation made him "angry and appalled", indicating that "When I joined the military, some 50 years ago, I swore an oath to support and defend the Constitution. Never did I dream that troops taking that same oath would be ordered under any circumstances to violate the constitutional rights of their fellow citizens—much less to provide a bizarre photo op for the elected Commander-in Chief, with military leadership standing alongside."

Freedom of Assembly is teetering on the brink, and likely will receive selective protection in the future based on which side of the political fence the demonstrators find themselves.

Denial of Right to Fair Trial.

The Sixth Amendment to the U.S. Constitution guarantees the rights of criminal defendants, including the right to a fair, public, speedy trial. The Due Process Clause extends these rights to the states as well. In America, anyone charged with a crime is entitled to legal representation, a public trial, and a jury of his or her peers. In our judicial system, a criminal defendant is presumed innocent until proven guilty. The Due Process Clause is intended to be a guarantee of justice and fundamental fairness, requiring:

- The government to provide clear and specific notice of the criminal charges based on the rule of law;
- An ability to show there is a clear standard of conduct which was violated by the criminal action;

- An opportunity to rebut the charges in a meaningful way, including the right to legal representation; and
- The government must establish that there is substantial and credible evidence supporting its charges.

These individual protections are not found in fascist nations, where "suspects" can be locked up (or worse) with no charges expressed and no opportunity to defend themselves. This fascist tendency has been demonstrated at numerous Trump rallies with chants of "lock her up" or comments from Trump himself in favor of jailing his political opponents or anyone who disagrees with him.

Elimination of these Constitutional protections, especially as they relate to suppression of political opposition by any means, including imprisonment or murder, would be a tragic and possibly irreversible step toward fascism in America.

Concentration of Wealth.

Inequality with respect to wealth is a "given" in nearly all forms of government throughout history. Even communism—a political ideology of equality-- has its elite classes with special privileges. The issue is not inequality. Rather, it is the level and extent of the gap between the "haves" and the "have-nots", and the role of politics and government in managing this inequality process.

An oligarchy provides an extreme form of concentration of wealth. It represents a governmental structure within a nation in which power vests in a small number of politically-connected people. Often, this privileged group exercises their power for greedy, corrupt purposes, aided and abetted by an autocratic leader.

Russia, and Russian-controlled puppet states, are examples of such plutocracies. Political patronage has resulted in oligarchs amassing untold wealth at the expense of the ordinary citizens. Autocratic favoritism provides ownership of important industries among a small, privileged class. The masses struggle to eke out a living, while the oligarchs and their families enjoy their yachts, private planes, dachas, foreign bank accounts, and elite university educations.

America has a long history of wealth inequality, based primarily on a system of capitalism and entrepreneurship. Much of the creation of wealth in America has been the result of opportunity, hard work, education, creativity, and dumb luck. Much of the concentration and growth of the wealth gap has been the result of privileged opportunities, slave labor, favorable tax laws, criminal activities, corruption, union-busting, and inter-generational gifts and inheritances.

The Trump Tax Reform Plan (aka "Trump's Big, Beautiful Tax Cut") of 2017 dramatically expanded the gap between haves and have-nots in America. Billionaire business owners effectively lobbied for a Plan that created maximum benefits to the wealthy. Top corporate tax rates were cut from 35% to 21%. The top individual rates dropped from 39.6% to 37%. Some of America's richest citizens (including Donald Trump) pay little or no federal income tax. As the wealth gap continues to expand in America, more and more economic power is falling into the hands of fewer and fewer people.

White Supremacy Movement.

The concept of a master race was the brain-child of Adolph Hitler. He deemed the putative "Aryan Race" to be the pinnacle of the human hierarchy. The Nazis declared that the Aryans were superior to all other races, giving them special privileges. To get an Aryan Certificate required citizens of Germany to trace their lineage by birth certificates, baptisms, or other certified proof that all grandparents and parents were of pure Aryan descent.

Slavs, Gypsies, and Jews were racially inferior by definition, and thus a danger to the master race. They were to be removed, expelled, enslaved, imprisoned, and murdered. All power--in government, military, business, professions, and society—rested in this privileged Aryan race.

Hitler's Nazi Germany is the model for white supremacist groups in America. Once considered politically incorrect in most parts of the U.S., these neo-nazis are re-appearing in the mainstream of American politics. An underlying fear of being replaced in power by dark-skinned citizens, non-Christians, Native Americans, Asian-Americans, and non-European immigrants appears to be the driving force for the American white supremacy movement.

As the anger and hatred generated by the white supremacists become accepted as the "new normal" in America, we become more and more vulnerable to fascist leadership that plays on those fears in order to rise to political power. It is a strategy of "divide and conquer."

Fascism feeds on fear, prejudice, anger, hatred, and racial division. The white supremacy movement is providing the necessary fuel.

Anti-Intellectualism.

There is a growing resistance in America to science and medicine that fails to match up with rationality and logic. The most recent example involves COVID-19, which has taken the lives of over a million Americans.

Despite a herculean and successful effort to develop vaccines to combat this once-in-a-century pandemic, vaccines have become a political football that is being kicked back and forth by the medical community, the vast majority of Americans, and a mostly far-right group of anti-vaxxers. Although the vaccines have proven to be incredibly effective in protecting people and limiting the spread of this highly contagious virus, some consider vaccines to be an infringement on individual rights. The theory is that the individual right not to be vaccinated trumps the individual responsibility not to spread this contagious disease to others.

One conspiracy theory is that the established medical community, the U.S. Government, and major drug companies are in cahoots to insert microchips into our bodies through the vaccines. The once-trusted medical and science communities are under attack.

Human-induced climate change has been irrefutably established by scientists around the world. Its effects are appearing everywhere, in the form of rising ocean levels, higher global temperatures, melting glaciers, and unprecedented storms, floods, and wildfires. The evidence of climate change is now indisputable, as is humanity's contribution to the problem. There is general agreement among scientists and governments on the steps that need to be taken to save Planet Earth from dying.

Notwithstanding the evidence, incredibly there are far-right politicians who continue to deny climate change. They know more than the scientists—and play on the fears of their constituencies.

A mistrust of the educational community is evident in angry outbursts at local school board meetings, protesting the teaching of black history, critical thinking, or gender education.

Tearing down the scientific, medical, and education communities is a step in the direction of fascism in America.

Patriotic Symbols.

Historically, flags have served as symbols of national pride. A fascination with historical or military flags, logos, and symbols seems to be a recurring theme of fascist movements. Fascist symbolism includes specific colors of military-like uniforms, such as Blackshirts and Brownshirts.

Mussolini's original symbol of fascism was the fasces—a bundle of sticks featuring an axe was an ancient Roman symbol of power over life and death. The color of the Blackshirts symbolized death. For many Italians under Mussolini, a coat of arms red chief with a fasces indicated an allegiance to the Fascist Party.

The Nazi Party under Hitler used the tan-brown uniforms of the SA paramilitary group as their identifying color. The swastika was a powerful symbol of the foundation of Germanic civilization, proclaiming that the Aryan race was the master race. "Blood and Soil" was a Nazi slogan proclaiming the idea of a pure Aryan race conquering territory for Germany. The Nazi stiff-arm salute had its origins in the Roman Empire. "Heil Hitler" was a ritual of the Hitler cult. Military marches and parades were a form of entertainment and intimidation during the Hitler Era.

Stalin's Hammer and Sickle was intended to represent the industrial working class and agricultural workers. The 5-pointed Red Star symbolized the triumph of the ideas of communism throughout the world.

Alt-right groups in America have adopted Mussolini's fasces in an apparent effort to connect their views with the bygone power of the Roman empire. White supremacist groups tend to favor

Hitler's symbols, including the swastika and phrases like "blood and soil". They also rely heavily on Confederate symbols such as the Confederate Flag. Trump's focus on symbolism includes flyovers by fighter jets, military parades, MAGA hats, and enveloping himself in the American flag.

Border Walls.

The Soviet Union was the best builder of walls since The Great Wall of China was built to fend off invaders. The U.S.S.R.'s walls, however, were in the form of an "iron curtain" to keep its citizens from escaping to freedom in the West.

A major theme of the Trump Era was to build a Mexican border wall so high and so impenetrable that no brown-skinned refugee fleeing violence in Central America could gain access to safety and freedom in America. Those refugees who made it through were detained, with families separated— children from their parents.

No such wall was proposed along the Canadian border to keep out the mostly white population of Canada. However, official immigration policy was changed to keep out Muslims and brown-skinned refugees from the Middle East.

The need for border walls in a global society intricately connected by commerce seems to be a relic of a fascist past.

Weakening of Checks and Balances.

In fascist nations, the autocratic ruler has absolute power to make policy decisions. There are no second opinions, or wise counsel from experienced and independent minds. Consensus building is not a part of the decision process. The result can be such disastrous unilateral decisions as Putin's invasion of Ukraine.

Simultaneous with the dysfunction and weakening of Congress, the Executive Branch of Government in Washington has assumed more and more power. Major policies are often the result of Executive Orders by the President. Military involvement, which used to be the domain of Congress, is now largely the role of the Commander in Chief.

With the loading of the Federal Judiciary with loyal, biased, ideological supporters of the President who appointed them to the Bench, the last check and balance in the American system is on the fence.

Schools as Tools for Indoctrination.

The public school system in America has been controversial for decades. Schools teach views that do not always match the views of parents or political officials. Some believe that schools indoctrinate young people with conservative attitudes; others believe schools are too liberal in their teachings. Some religious groups are appalled that religion and Christianity are not part of the public-school curriculum.

In recent years schools have become a battle ground over such issues as:

- Should students (and teachers) be required to wear masks to prevent the spread of COVID-19?
- Is requiring COVID vaccinations in schools a violation of individual rights?
- Is it appropriate to teach the history of race in America?
- May sex/gender education be a part the lesson plan?
- Which books are appropriate to ban from the eyes of curious students?
- Is the teaching of critical thinking a dangerous policy?
- Is Holocaust Denial a proper approach to protect young students from learning about an unfortunate phase of world history?

Public schools have become a political football, with school boards, teachers, and administrators literally under attack for providing educational opportunities that scare some parents. The attitude appears to be that parents, not professional educators, should be determining the lesson plans for the students.

Private schools have flourished in this political environment, allowing for the inclusion of religious education and conservative values during the school day. A significant portion of the funding of public schools has been re-directed to the private school system. Re-segregation of the school system is well underway, with public schools peopled largely by black and brown students, and private schools mostly white.

As this process unfolds, the opportunity for teaching unquestioning students continues to grow. As evidenced by the Hitler Youth, young students can be easy picking for a fascist government.

Part Three. Responses to the Threat of Fascism in America.

"Acts of kindness have an impact far beyond the act itself. When I am kind, helpful, or respectful to someone, I feel good about myself and exude positive energy, lightness, and joy. The recipient of my kindness feels blessed and treats his or her family or friends with loving kindness. Family members and friends are infected with this kindness virus, and pass it on to others. Before long, a pandemic of goodwill is spread far and wide—a ripple effect all due to the seed of one simple act of kindness." Jim Boeglin, Seeds of Kindness in a Time of Crisis

It is my belief that the vast majority of Americans do not prefer to live in a fascist State. I have not witnessed a surge of American emigres defecting to Russia, or China, or North Korea, or Iran. Most Americans rightly see fascism as a closed, dark, cruel, controlling, and regimented form of government that suppresses the rights, freedoms, and values of its citizens. Yet, it continues to make inroads into American society and politics. There must be a reason for fascism's current rise in popularity in America.

The initial step to addressing this threat is obvious. There needs to be an awakening within the American people—an awareness of the fascist threat. It is not yet widely recognized that the threat to democracy comes from within. As Pogo would say, "We have met the enemy, and he is us." *Walt Kelly.*

Some Americans consider democracy to be morally inferior to an authoritarian system. In fact, I believe some white evangelical Christians prefer a system in which one party and one white male leader has total power over the conduct of the nation.

The belief among these radical right groups is that far too many people have access to the ballot box. They feel that a government by and for the people has led America morally astray, as evidenced by popular support for abortions, birth control, same sex marriage, LGBTQ rights, diversity, multicultural values, toleration of non-Christian religions, welfare programs, immigration policies, and the general breakdown of traditional Christian family values. Their answer to this perceived moral decay in America is an authoritarian form of government.

This book is intended to be a tiny piece of the awakening to the growing threat within America to our democratic form of government. Beyond the awareness, however, resolution of the threat is going to take wide-spread action and determination. It is relatively easy to write or talk about the threat of fascism. It is quite another matter to effectively address the threat and offer solutions.

In my opinion, it is going to take a collective effort of the American people to resolve the threat of fascism. Unlike Donald Trump's autocratic claim that "I alone can fix it", not one person or one think tank or one circle of wise elders can fix this problem alone. Systemic changes are needed that require the participation of all concerned Americans from every diverse background. A shift in the collective consciousness is required—from fear, anger, and hatred, to trust and loving kindness.

There is a timeless spiritual principle that what we put out into the world is what we get back. If we emit anger, disrespect, hatred, and bias, that is pretty much what our world will look like. If we emit kindness, caring, understanding, and empathy, that is what comes back into our world. Some people call this karma, others refer to giving and receiving being the same thing. We have the power to create a paradigm shift in America and the world. That shift begins with me—and with you. Neither of us can do it alone.

There is a tendency among human beings to focus on effects and largely ignore their causes. It's like the adage that I can give a person a fish, and he can eat for a day. It's an easy short-term answer to hunger pangs. Or, I can teach a person to fish, and he can eat for a lifetime. This is a more complex effort addressing the cause of the hunger, but with long-term ramifications. Another way of thinking of it is:

- All human behavior is deeply rooted in thoughts, feelings, and emotions;
- Traditionally, we have often treated the behavior (symptoms) instead of the causes (thoughts and feelings at the underlying root of the behavior);
- Treating the symptoms can make a difference, but it rarely resolves the problem in the long run. (For example, locking up criminals may protect society during the term of incarceration, but treating attitudes and conditions that foster crime can have real and long-term consequences);
- The underlying causes are often invisible, hidden, disguised, or misrepresented;
- As such, treating cause can be a difficult and complex process.

We see this tendency in treatment of addictions, or psychological issues, or controlling inappropriate or abusive behavior. Programs designed to uncover the root of the problem tend to be more effective in the long run than the programs designed to modify or medicate the behavior.

I believe the most effective way to address the symptoms of fascism is to acknowledge and treat the underlying causes that give rise to the appeal of fascism in the first place.

Attitudes that Promote Fascism, and their Antidotes.

By attitude, I mean a person's settled way of thinking or feeling toward someone, something, or life in general. Attitudes establish values, individually or within a group. By definition, attitudes are entrenched and difficult to change. Collective attitudes of a group or clan or gang are close to impossible to change.

Many mental health professionals believe that thoughts and emotions underlying all attitudes are a manifestation of either fear or love. Angry, hateful, deceptive, greedy, violent, abusive attitudes are generally rooted in fear. Kindness, tolerance, respect, integrity, fairness, trust, empathy, inner peace, understanding, generosity, and forgiveness are fueled by love. Letting go of fears and moving in the direction of love can be a life-long journey.

America is currently home to opposing and polarizing attitudes. The willingness of political parties, families, communities, churches, and diverse cultures to work together is an essential step for healing these opposing forces. It is not a matter of one side "winning over" the other side, but rather reaching an understanding of each other's goals and fears, and determining the common needs and the common goals of the whole. It is only with this understanding and goodwill that a paradigm shift is possible. Such a shift is beyond our reach so long as the preferred approach is to attack and defend. Any attack just entrenches the attitude and exacerbates the problem.

Releasing Anger and Hatred.

There is no shortage of anger and hatred in American society. Its symptoms include gun violence, road rage, political nastiness, attacks on school boards, disrespect of authority, bullying, gang warfare, racial bias against minorities and immigrants, denial of history and science, incivility, vigilante justice, social media attacks, spreading unfounded conspiracy theories, child abuse, spousal abuse, gender abuse, and mean-spirited attacks on each other. All of this anger and hatred—fueled by fear—provides fertile ground for the growth of fascism in America.

There is also a great deal of kindness, generosity, tolerance, courtesy, and respect in America. Its symptoms include being open and welcoming to diverse groups, neighbor helping neighbor, stranger helping stranger, random acts of kindness, charitable giving, reacting non-defensively to an angry attack, caring for a person in need, volunteering at a soup kitchen or homeless shelter, and treating everyone with courtesy and respect. All of these symptoms— fueled by love—offer hope for the future of American democracy and the demise of the fascist threat.

It is unlikely that all anger and hate in America will be eradicated in my lifetime, but there are daily opportunities for ordinary Americans to push the envelope in the direction of a kinder and gentler society. Modeling loving kindness may penetrate the consciousness of some family members, friends, or neighbors, influencing them to question their own behaviors and underlying attitudes and fears.

Light does not attack darkness; it shines it away. Lending a non-judgmental hand to a person in trouble can transform a relationship. Reacting to an unkind remark with loving kindness can change the personal dynamics. With each act of kindness, the circle of love expands and shines away some of the anger and hatred. To paraphrase Benito Mussolini, it is putting the feathers of democracy back on the chicken, one feather at a time.

Learning to be Non-Defensive.

"If you are not kind to unkind people, you are one of them. Unconditional kindness is not a declaration of who deserves it, it's a declaration of who you are. Ancient Buddhist Wisdom

It seems to be human nature to react to perceived bad behavior with anger, judgment, and counter-attack. It is a knee-jerk reaction of the ego that may feel good at the time. Sometimes it is difficult to remember that we have a choice how to react to mean-spiritedness. Modeling appropriate behavior in response to inappropriate behavior is always an available option.

Reacting non-defensively to mean-spirited attacks may lead to understandings rather than to animosity, confrontation, further personal attacks, and violence. There is an ancient spiritual principle that our safety lies in being defenseless. It takes more than one person to do battle.

What we see in another person we are likely to see in ourselves. What we give out, we are likely to receive back. The surest way to be treated with love and respect is to be loving and respectful to everyone else in our lives—even when someone's behavior falls short of our expectations.

Fascism is a concept based on fear, which generates anger, hatred, mistruths, and power over others. Its fearful symptoms include bigotry, greed, false propaganda, hypocrisy, personal attacks, suppression, oppression, and divisiveness.

Fighting against the symptoms of fascism has traditionally fueled the fire, leading to violent confrontations and destructive energies. Historically, fighting the symptoms of fascism hasn't worked very well—unless "winning" a protracted, bloody, destructive war with millions of human casualties is considered a successful result.

Listening to Learn.

One of *Stephen Covey's* seven habits for highly effective people is: Seek first to understand...then to be understood. It appears to be human nature to reverse this process. When I "know" I'm right, what's the point of listening to another perspective? For most of us, it is more important for other people to understand our position than it is to actively listen in order to deeply understand someone else's position. We want to be right, even if it destroys a relationship. Our egos would rather be right than have to listen to another perspective.

Learning to actively listen does not mean that we must agree with the other person. Rather, it allows us to respond respectfully and with acknowledgment, insight, and understanding. This can be the beginning of a meaningful dialogue that leads to resolution of the underlying disagreement, rather than an angry argument that leads to damaged relationships.

Nowhere is this need to listen greater than in today's political discussions, which have torn apart families and communities. We have a choice. We can assume the "enemy" is stupid, insane, mistaken; or we can carefully listen in order to understand where they are coming from. Only then can we appreciate that they are fellow human beings, and participate in a discussion that can lead to healing.

From Judging to Understanding.

Humans are quick to form opinions about other human beings. We tend to label people based on such superficial features as physical appearance, height, weight, color of skin, style of clothing, athletic ability, intelligence, education, size of house, car ownership, church affiliation, social memberships, age, gender identification, political leaning, etc. We have become quite good at pigeon-holing the people in our lives.

Judgments are a function of our egos. It is seeing one another as physical beings, in competition with each other for limited resources. It is comparing everyone else with our own self-image. Is he/she smarter than me, better looking than me, richer than me? It is quite easy to completely overlook the essence of the person "under the hood."

Seeing others through ego eyes causes us to see ourselves through this same limiting filter. Am I rich enough, smart enough, handsome enough? Focused on the surface, it is nearly impossible to discover who I really am.

We can only understand another person (or ourselves for that matter) if we are willing to withhold judgments, and get to know the person deep inside. We can only bridge divides with a willingness to listen and understand.

From Incivility to Respect.

One need only look to Congress for a model of incivility in America. These democratically-elected "leaders" are demonstrating attitudes and behaviors that would not be tolerated in most American families, businesses, churches, social organizations, or schools. Trumpism makes it acceptable for politicians to be hypocritical, untruthful, and just plain nasty attack dogs. It is not a good model for a nation that is already vulnerable to being angry and fearful.

This disrespect and incivility has filtered down from The White House and Capitol Hill to state legislatures, governors' mansions, town halls, school board meetings, community organizations, sporting events, law enforcement agencies, corporate boardrooms, the workplace, classrooms, political parties, election officials, and social media. Incivility and disrespect are rapidly becoming the norm in America.

It should not be surprising that murders, mass shootings, book-banning, and abusive personal attacks are on the rise. It should also not be surprising that fascism is gaining adherents in America on the theme of law and order.

Civility and respect go hand in hand. Civility involves genuine behavior that is polite, courteous, and respectful to everyone—friend or foe. Like incivility, civility is contagious. When people are treated with respect, they reciprocate. Democracies are built on civility, mutual respect, and cooperation. Fascism is built on incivility, disrespect, raw power, and absolute control.

It is admittedly a challenge to be respectful to someone behaving like an ass. It is not easy to look beyond the behavior to the inner essence of the fearful actor. I believe that, if we want our democracy to survive, it is essential that sane Americans pull themselves out of the gutter of contempt and re-learn how to function with loving kindness. It has to start somewhere. Why not here?

From Hypocrisy to Authenticity.

When a person's behavior is inconsistent or contradictory to stated beliefs, that person is known as a hypocrite. For most of human history, hypocritical behavior has been considered shameful. In the past, obvious hypocrisy was an embarrassing kiss of death for a political career. It denoted insincerity, or even stupidity. Hypocrisy was not an admired behavior for anyone, regardless of position.

To most people, hypocrisy feels phony or fake. Most of us prefer authenticity to hypocrisy. We like being with people who are real, genuine, honest, trustworthy, and sincere. Within ourselves, hypocrisy destroys self-esteem. Authenticity, on the other hand, increases self-esteem and self-confidence.

When highly functioning people observe hypocritical behavior in politicians, it diminishes trust in the politician and sometimes the entire political system. In recent years, the shame of political hypocrisy has evolved into acceptable political strategy for some of our elected "leaders". It is a phenomenon that is spreading distrust of a government run by elected officials.

When a representative form of government wallows in hypocrisy, the idea of autocracy naturally gains attraction for some. When elected leaders would rather spread ruinous lies than build consensus for the common good, authoritarianism will inevitably be on the rise.

Before hypocritical politicians can be held accountable for their destructive behavior, voters must be willing to recognize and acknowledge the disease. Our elected officials may be a reflection of the collective consciousness of American society. As long as a majority of voters admire and respect hypocritical behavior, our representative form of government is in danger.

Hypocrisy needs to be addressed at the grass roots level. Only when political leaders learn that hypocritical behavior is not acceptable to their constituency will authenticity return to government. The collective consciousness needs to make this paradigm shift. It cannot happen without our participation.

Personal Integrity.

People of integrity have nothing to hide. They have strong moral beliefs and tend to live lives based on values, principles, and a consistency of righteous actions. A person of integrity travels a consistent path for making decisions so that other people know that he or she will be measured, sane, and sensible, no matter the situation. Values will always prevail.

Personal integrity has not been a treasured value in American politics during the Trump Era. Deceptions, half-truths, and hidden motives have been all too common. People who should know better have been willing to "sell their souls" to remain in the good graces of an autocratic leader. The moral principle of "true north" has meandered south, east, and west. Not surprisingly, authoritarianism has left its cult-like followers morally weak.

Ironically, the very religious institutions that preach and teach personal integrity are willing to give this moral principle a pass for political purposes. Too many Christians are willing to "talk the talk" of personal integrity, but are reluctant to "walk the walk." They are willing to overlook their own values and principles for political objectives. That does not bode well for the future of personal integrity—or for American democracy.

Nazi Germany learned this lesson the hard way. Many German citizens were willing to "turn a blind eye" to Hitler's inexcusable treatment of Jews and other "inferior" members of society. They put their personal integrity aside, thereby choosing Hitler's cruel vision of a master race. It didn't work out very well for anyone in Germany in the 1930s and 1940s.

Unless and until personal integrity makes a comeback in America, we remain vulnerable to a powerful, opportunistic, and amoral leader taking us down the road to fascism. This comeback can only happen by a shift of attitude in churches, schools, families, businesses, clubs, social media, and individual voters. A shift toward personal integrity could indeed Make America Great Again.

From Resentment to Forgiveness.

As a recovering Catholic, I've learned that forgiveness is a much deeper topic than the confessional box. It has to begin with forgiving ourselves. We cannot give something we don't possess. Until we are willing to forgive ourselves, it is doubly difficult to forgive someone else.

Forgiveness is not an ego-value. The ego would much rather hold onto feelings of resentment or indignation for how we've been mistreated. Unfortunately, failure to forgive is like shooting one's self in the foot.

When a political system has as its foundation an attitude of resentment and non-forgiveness, it has a tendency to lose respect for the rule of law. America has witnessed this attitude domestically during the Trump Era. Trump will never forgive American voters for stealing his election, even though every court in the land has demonstrated that the

American voters did no such thing. My educated guess is that for the past seven decades Donald Trump has not forgiven a single person for a real or alleged slight. He holds onto his resentments, and considers himself special and above the law. Trump will likely never accept the decisions of the courts with respect to his defeat. His ego will not allow it.

The world has witnessed flagrant disrespect for international law during the Putin Era. Putin's long-held resentment over the decades-old political breakup of the Soviet Union sparked the brutal and illegal military invasion of Ukraine. Putin valued his resentments more than he valued international law that requires respect for the borders of neighboring countries. As dictator, he considered himself above international law.

Authoritarian power tends to take precedence over legal protections, justified by resentment of the "enemy". Fascism is all about replacing the rule of law with the rule of raw power.

We were given a model for forgiveness by the surviving victims and relatives of the Charleston massacre. In a vicious hate crime based on race, a twenty-one-year-old white supremacist, Dylann Roof, murdered nine black members of Emanuel African Methodist Episcopal Church in Charleston, South Carolina. Many of the people directly affected by this hate crime chose to forgive the young shooter. By forgiving a white supremacist, they were able to free themselves from the resentment and hatred that could have held themselves captive for the rest of their lives.

Clearly, forgiving is much more difficult than holding onto a resentment. Forgiveness is not for the weak. Forgiveness requires courage. In the end, however, the primary beneficiary of forgiveness is the forgiver, now free to move forward.

America can learn from the Charleston model. That would be a step in the direction of choosing democracy over fascism.

From Supremacy to Equality.

Critical Race Theory is the study of the history of oppression of black people in America. It is an opportunity to reflect on the inequality in America's past, so that we may become a better nation in the future. Acknowledging our past is a critical element for a better future.

White supremacy is a misguided, superficial movement that is barely skin-deep. It is a movement based on fear. Ironically, these misguided folks are proving a point—that anyone believing in the value of a human being based on color of skin is functioning at an extremely low level. They might be better served by arguing for equality.

Hitler's treatment of Jews and other so-called inferior races was intended to raise the Aryan race to a master level. In fact, it did just the opposite. The activities of Hitler and his Aryan followers brought the German nation and its master race to ignominious defeat and ruin.

Most Christians have been taught better than to believe in racial supremacy. It appears that some members of the flock slept through those sermons. For Christians to believe that color of skin is the determiner of human worth is to ignore the teachings of Jesus—himself a brown-skinned person.

Equality does not mean that every person in America has the same talents or abilities. It does mean that every person has the same rights, privileges, and opportunities, and is entitled to be treated with respect without regard to race, gender preference, religion, age, or national origin.

Democracy thrives in atmospheres of equality; fascism thrives in attitudes of supremacy.

From Lies to Truth.

Honesty and truthfulness have been long-standing American traditions that have become recent casualties of political partisanship. Lying can be outright, or half-truths intended to deceive. Whichever form it takes, mis-truths are destroying trust in our democratic form of government.

I understand that the truth is not identical for everyone. We all tend to perceive reality through filters that have formed over our life experiences. Because we have all been subjected to different experiences, we all see truth from a slightly different angle. However, deep down, we know when we are being truthful or not.

The essence of dishonesty is not necessarily the actual words or actions. Rather, it is the intent behind them. When Vladimir Putin said the buildup of military resources on the border of Ukraine was not for the purpose of invading his neighbor, he intended to mislead Ukraine and the world. When he described the invasion as an "ongoing military operation" and banned Russian journalists and citizens from using terms like "invasion". "Attack", or "war", Putin's intent was to mislead the Russian people.

Donald Trump has an unbroken string of lies about every conceivable subject, from his political positions prior to his presidency, to the size of his crowds, to the extent of his wealth, to the frequency of his appearances on the cover of Time Magazine, to taking credit for actions that preceded him, to blaming others for things he did, to criminal accusations of his political opponents, to his golf scores, to fraud in his non-election. We can only imagine the mistruths that would arise if he was in a totalitarian, authoritarian position.

America has come to expect and accept lies. Untruths have reared their ugly heads in government, politics, business, religion, schools, sports, social media, the press, and personal relationships. One sure way to Make America Great Again would be to bring truthfulness and honesty back into fashion in the American Consciousness.

There are many Americans (perhaps the majority) who are basically honest and truthful. This group needs to become the foundation for spreading the message, restoring a culture in which truthfulness is an admired and honorable way of life. The survival of our representative form of government may depend on us.

Closing Thoughts

From 20th Century history and 21st Century experience, we know more or less what a fascist American State might look like. We suspect it would involve anger, fear, brutal suppression of individual rights, totalitarian control by one person or party, cruel oppression or elimination of "inferior" groups, impenetrable border walls, deceptive propaganda from a state-controlled media, nationalistic attitudes, military involvement in civil matters, voter suppression, oligarchs and a tremendous wealth gap, dictatorial decision making, and a political police force focused on protecting the interests of the autocratic elite at the expense of the people.

The opposite of a fascist State is what I think of as a Freedom State. It is a nation-state that is open and welcoming, diverse, interdependent and cooperative with other nations, peaceful, respectful, civil, generous, working together for the common good, with equal justice and opportunity for all.

Transformation often happens as a result of an external stimulus. For example, Putin's inhumane invasion of Ukraine appears to have unified and galvanized an often-divided international community to cooperate at new levels. A serious health challenge can cause a whole new lifestyle or way of thinking. The experience of a painful divorce can lead to new understandings and higher levels of functioning in relationships. Death of a loved one may generate spiritual and emotional growth for the survivors.

Transformation can also happen from the inside out, without an external force involved. It can be an inner decision to become pro-active, eliminate a negative habit, change an attitude, learn a new skill, or to see things differently.

As food for thought, I have written a series of poems in the form of questions. As the author of two books of poetry on the subject of Kindness, I feel able to express my thoughts best in poem form. These poems are intended to re-focus our inner consciousness on transforming America from the inside out. Transformation from an angry, divided nation in the direction of a grace-filled State of Freedom and Justice for all.

Grace.

What if kindness, poise, and grace
Prevailed in leadership,
Free of fear or saving face,
Replaced by kindly Statesmanship?
Would voters come to appreciate
Domed chambers hard at work,
No time for nastiness and hate--
No need to be a jerk?

Trust.

What if facts were the foundation
For political decisions--
No spin or lies or confrontations
Fueling personal ambitions?
Might truth and trust prevail
In policy positions,
A whole new form of holy grail
Guiding a new kind of politician?

Justice.

What if equal justice is the goal
No matter color of skin—
Regardless rich or on the dole,
Or bloodlines thick or thin?
Would the bloody anger we have seen
From injustice far and wide

Finally exit the nation's scene
Causing tempers to subside?

Integrity.

What if each one of us decides
Based on principles and values,
With never a need to lie or hide,
And only truth from which to choose?
What if deceit is cast aside
And truth is back in style,
Might integrity heal divides,
And bridge across the aisle?

Courage.

What if courage is standing up
For what we know is right?
The bravery to interrupt
Cold darkness with warm light!
Overcoming daunting fears
To speak when all alone,
A solo voice among the jeers
That sets a higher tone.

Respect.

What if kindness and respect
Were unleashed upon the Land?
Would they have the effect

To grow and to expand?
Might disrespect become a trait
That all but disappears,
A dinosaur like fear and hate,
Rejected by our peers?

Peace.

What if conflict, fear, and strife
Met with their demise,
Victims of a heartfelt life
That's peaceful, true, and wise?
Would we miss the nastiness
That fear and hatred bring?
Or would we treasure peacefulness,
In a tranquil world with wings?

Hope.

What if life is expectations
That our inner thoughts create,
Fulfilling all our aspirations,
Whether lowly hate, or a loving state?
Would we choose to focus on fear
If we knew we had a choice?
Wouldn't hope become the clear
Direction of our voice?

Authenticity.

What if genuine and real
Were traits that we admire?
Would we make a bigger deal
Out of leaders who are liars?
Might this be the time to make
The choice for sincerity;
To cast a vote to oust the fakes,
Replaced by authenticity?

Wisdom.

What if light and understanding
Arise from open minds?
What if ignorance is expanding
In darkness that's designed
To hide those fearful attitudes
That bring us to the brink?
Those dark and stormy moods
That discourage us to think.

About the Author

Fascism in the 21st Century is Jim's sixth book. A retired attorney, Jim began his writing career in 2017 at the age of 74 with The Bike Writer—lessons learned along the bicycle paths of life. It was a sharing of his life experiences and philosophies. He followed up a year later with Character Building, and then American Values in the Trump Era.

During the COVID-19 Pandemic, Jim chose poetry for Seeds of Kindness in a Time of Crisis, and Discovering Kindness in a Deeply Divided World. Fascism in the 21st Century is a return to prose, with just a hint of poetry as food for thought.

During the Pandemic, Jim and his wife, Jan, moved from their twenty-year experience in Bonita Springs, FL, back to their former hometown of Fort Wayne, IN, to be close to family and old friends. Golfing, hiking, and biking are now seasonal pastimes, leaving more time for Jim to write.

CPSIA information can be obtained
at www.ICGtesting.com
Printed in the USA
JSHW041942240822
29559JS00002B/77